**Women in Sports**

# ABBY WAMBACH

by Esther Porter

CAPSTONE PRESS
a capstone imprint

Pebble Plus is published by Capstone Press
1710 Roe Crest Drive, North Mankato, Minnesota 56003
www.mycapstone.com

**Library of Congress Cataloging-in-Publication Data**
Cataloging-in-Publication Data is on file with the Library of Congress.
ISBN 978-1-4914-7974-2 (library binding)
ISBN 978-1-4914-8570-5 (paperback)
ISBN 978-1-4914-8576-7 (eBook PDF)

**Editorial Credits**
Abby Colich, editor; Sarah Bennett, designer; Eric Gohl, media researcher;
Katy LaVigne, production specialist

**Photo Credits**
Alamy: Colin Underhill, 7; Dreamstime: Flight69, cover (background), 1; Getty Images:
FIFA/Stuart Franklin, 19; Newscom: Icon SMI/Howard C. Smith, 13, Icon SMI/Isaac
Menashe, 11, Reuters/Fabrizio Bensch, 17, USA Today Sports/Bruce Fedyck, cover, ZUMA
Press/Carl Sandin, 5, ZUMA Press/George Tiedemann, 15, ZUMA Press/Vaughn Ridley,
21; Shutterstock: hxdbzxy, 9 (background), 22, Pincarel, 3, 23, SOMKKU, back cover, 2, 24;
University of Florida/Athletic Association: 9

## Note to Parents and Teachers

The Women in Sports set supports national curriculum standards for social
studies related to people, places, and culture. This book describes and illustrates
Abby Wambach. The images support early readers in understanding the text. The
repetition of words and phrases helps early readers learn new words. This book
also introduces early readers to subject-specific vocabulary words, which are
defined in the Glossary section. Early readers may need assistance to read some
words and to use the Table of Contents, Glossary, Read More, Internet Sites, Critical
Thinking Using the Common Core, and Index sections of the book.

Printed in the United States of America in North Mankato, Minnesota.
092015 009221CGS16

# Table of Contents

# A Family of Athletes

Abby Wambach was born

June 2, 1980. She was

the youngest of seven children.

Her sister Beth liked soccer.

Soon Abby was playing the sport.

**TIMELINE**

1980

born in Rochester,
New York

Abby joined her first
soccer team at age 4.
In high school she was
a skilled player. She scored
142 goals in four years.

**TIMELINE**

| 1980 | 1994 | 1998 |

born in Rochester, New York

begins playing high school soccer

finishes high school with 142 goals

# Rising Star

After high school Abby played for the University of Florida. She helped her team win its first national title. Abby became the school's all-time top scorer.

**TIMELINE**

1980 — born in Rochester, New York

1994 — begins playing high school soccer

1998 — finishes high school with 142 goals

wins national title with the University of Florida

From 2002 to 2003, Abby played for the Washington Freedom. She was Rookie of the Year in 2002. Her team won the WUSA title in 2003. Abby was the MVP.

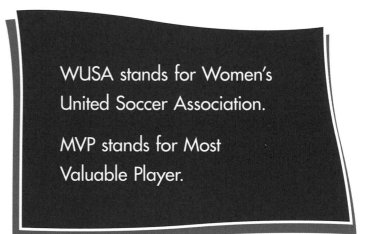

WUSA stands for Women's United Soccer Association.

MVP stands for Most Valuable Player.

**TIMELINE**

| 1980 | 1994 | 1998 | 2002 | 2003 |
|---|---|---|---|---|
| born in Rochester, New York | begins playing high school soccer | finishes high school with 142 goals | begins playing for the Washington Freedom | wins title with the Washington Freedom and is MVP |
| | | wins national title with the University of Florida | | |

Abby played in the World Cup in 2003. She led the United States to the bronze medal. Abby was named U.S. Soccer Female Athlete of the Year. She won this award seven more times.

**TIMELINE**

| 1980 | 1994 | 1998 | 2002 | 2003 |
| --- | --- | --- | --- | --- |
| born in Rochester, New York | begins playing high school soccer | finishes high school with 142 goals | begins playing for the Washington Freedom | wins title with the Washington Freedom and is MVP |
| | | wins national title with the University of Florida | | wins World Cup bronze medal |

13

Abby played for the United States in the 2004 Olympics. The team won gold. Abby played in another World Cup in 2007. The U.S. team again won a bronze medal.

## TIMELINE

**1980**
born in Rochester, New York

**1994**
begins playing high school soccer

**1998**
finishes high school with 142 goals

wins national title with the University of Florida

**2002**
begins playing for the Washington Freedom

**2003**
wins title with the Washington Freedom and is MVP

wins World Cup bronze medal

2004

wins gold at
the Olympics

2007

wins World Cup
bronze medal

# Unstoppable

Abby shined at the World Cup in 2011. She scored a last-minute head shot against Brazil. The goal was voted best in Women's World Cup history. The U.S. team won the silver medal.

## TIMELINE

**1980**
born in Rochester, New York

**1994**
begins playing high school soccer

**1998**
finishes high school with 142 goals

wins national title with the University of Florida

**2002**
begins playing for the Washington Freedom

**2003**
wins title with the Washington Freedom and is MVP

wins World Cup bronze medal

2004
wins gold at
the Olympics

2007
wins World Cup
bronze medal

2011
head shot against
Brazil voted best
in Women's World
Cup history

17

Abby was named the Women's
World Player of the Year
in 2012. Then she played
in her second Olympics.
The U.S. team again won gold.

**TIMELINE**

1980
born in Rochester,
New York

1994
begins playing high
school soccer

1998
finishes high school with
142 goals

wins national title with
the University of Florida

2002
begins playing for the
Washington Freedom

2003
wins title with the
Washington Freedom
and is MVP

wins World Cup
bronze medal

**2004**
wins gold at
the Olympics

**2007**
wins World Cup
bronze medal

**2011**
head shot against
Brazil voted best
in Women's World
Cup history

**2012**
named Women's World
Player of the Year

wins gold at
the Olympics

Abby broke a world record
in 2013. She had scored more
goals than any female or male.
Abby's last World Cup was
in 2015. She finally won gold.

## TIMELINE

**1980**
born in Rochester,
New York

**1994**
begins playing high
school soccer

**1998**
finishes high school with
142 goals

wins national title with
the University of Florida

**2002**
begins playing for the
Washington Freedom

**2003**
wins title with the
Washington Freedom
and is MVP

wins World Cup
bronze medal

| 2004 | 2007 | 2011 | 2012 | 2013 | 2015 |
|------|------|------|------|------|------|
| wins gold at the Olympics | wins World Cup bronze medal | head shot against Brazil voted best in Women's World Cup history | named Women's World Player of the Year

wins gold at the Olympics | breaks world record for most goals scored | wins the World Cup |

# Glossary

**head shot**—in soccer, the act of hitting the ball with the head to try to score a goal

**MVP**—short for Most Valuable Player; an award that goes to the best player in a game or season

**record**—when something is done better than anyone has ever done it before

**rookie**—a first-year player or participant

**title**—an award given to the winner of a tournament

# Read More

**Bankston, John.** *Abby Wambach.* Blue Banner Biographies. Hockessin, Del.: Mitchell Lane Publishers, 2014.

**Fishman, Jon M.** *Abby Wambach.* Amazing Athletes. Minneapolis: Lerner Publications, 2014.

**Jökulsson, Illugi.** *Stars of Women's Soccer.* World Soccer Legends. New York: Abbeville Press, 2015.

# Internet Sites

FactHound offers a safe, fun way to find Internet sites related to this book. All of the sites on FactHound have been researched by our staff.

Here's all you do:
Visit *www.facthound.com*
Type in this code: 9781491479742

Super-cool stuff! Check out projects, games and lots more at
**www.capstonekids.com**

## Critical Thinking Using the Common Core

1. Reread page 4. What might be different if Abby's sister was interested in a sport other than soccer? (Integration of Knowledge and Ideas)

2. Page 16 says Abby's head shot was voted the best goal in Women's World Cup history. Use the glossary to describe what a head shot is. (Craft and Structure)

## Index